First time in Italy

Sergio Néster

Short and really useful manual
with practical advice and secrets
from locals

+ necessary phrases in Italian
for various situations

Made in Italy

Text: Sergio Néster
Illustrator: Natasha Bo. / Editor: Sviatlana Papova
Tech. Specialist: N. Monroe
Language adaptation: Nathan Loy

Since you've bought this book, you've probably decided to visit Italy. If it's your first time, I'm even a little envious of you.

You know, the first time is absolutely amazing. Not that it's bad afterwards — the second, third, and fourth times are great too. Italy is so diverse that you can count for a long time.

But still, the first time is the first time. And it's also the most challenging. It's unclear how things work, what to do and what not to do, what's right and what's wrong. Much is not very clear if you're in Italy for the first time.

This book is written so that you fall in love with this place, and after the first time, there will be a second, third, fourth, and fifth time. The fifth wasn't enough for me, so I decided to move to Italy for good. I hope my experience of living in Italy, which is shared in this book, will be useful to you.

This book is for you. For your First Time.

First time in Italy

—

Contents

Chapter 1

What is Italy?

You know, there are people who read books starting from the middle. They just open somewhere in the middle and read a random chapter. It's very good that you're not one of them. Now I'll tell you why.

Because this is the most important chapter in the book. If you have absolutely no time for reading, just read this chapter, and you'll read the others when you have time. Which probably means never, right? :)

Okay, I'm sure you're not ready to skip 11 chapters about the most beautiful country in the world, which you seem to be planning to visit. Or at least want to learn a little more about it.

So, here's what I want to tell you: Italy doesn't actually exist. Yes, it's just as you read it: Italy does not exist. There is a piece of land in the Mediterranean Sea that strikingly resembles a boot. I don't really like it when the beautiful Apennine Peninsula is called a boot. But it does look like one, I must admit.

So, what exists if not Italy? There are 20 different countries that are situated on the boot-shaped peninsula. Sometimes they resemble each other, and sometimes they are completely different, so much so that it's even incorrect to compare them. It's like saying that the Netherlands and France are one country.

Why is that? Because just 150 years ago, Italy consisted of 20 separate territories until one bearded man, whose name you'll hear more than once, decided to unite them. I won't bore you with historical excursions, if you're interested you can read about it on Wikipedia. I'll just say that the bearded man's name was Giuseppe Garibaldi, and he is a national hero of Italy. As I said, you'll hear his name again, almost every Italian city has a street or square named after Giuseppe Garibaldi.

What does all this mean for you? It means that it's important where exactly in Italy you are. Depending on this, much changes: from the peculiarities of cuisine to an almost non-Italian language and a different temperament of the locals. Well, we'll come back to that.

▶ *How do you determine where Northern Italy ends and Southern Italy begins? Look to Rome: everything located above Rome can be conditionally considered Northern Italy and eeverything below it is Southern Italy*

Some Italian phrases you may need to be friendly in Italy

Ciao [CHOW]
Hi / Bye

Buongiorno [bwon-JOHR-noh]
Good afternoon

Buonasera [bwon-ah-SEH-rah]
Good evening

Arrivederci [ah-ree-veh-DEHR-chee]
Goodbye

Grazie [GRAHT-see-eh]
Thank you

Prego [PREH-goh]
Please (in response to thank you)

Per favore [pair fah-VOH-ray]
Please (upon request)

Mi scusi [mee SKOO-see]
Excuse me

Signore / Signora [seen-YOH-ray/ /seen-YOH-rah]
Sir / Madam (when addressed)

Chapter 2

South vs. North

Now let's try to decide whether to explore the South or the North of Italy.

Anyone even slightly familiar with the history of the United States knows about the North-South conflict that took place 150 years ago.

United Italy is also about 150 years old, and there are still some tensions between the North and the South, even to this day. The only difference is that the Southerners don't want slavery — quite the opposite.

Residents of Southern Italy often don't demonstrate a huge desire to build a career, they're not in a hurry to go anywhere, and they don't try to earn all the money in the world. In the South of Italy, people rarely come to meetings on time (this also applies to public transport) and don't get annoyed if someone is late. The life of the Italian South is filled with warm chaos, leisurely conversations, and simple pleasures. Here they value pasta, the sea, and free time.

Northerners have nothing against pasta either, but they definitely have less free time. In Northern Italy, historically, there's been less chaos and more order. And slightly strained relations with the South.

Let's briefly go back to post-war Italy. Don't worry, there won't be any long, boring lectures. This is just to help you understand the context. I'll be very concise.

In the 50s-60s, Italy experienced what is often called an economic miracle, and this miracle happened mainly in Northern Italy because this is where all the industrial power was concentrated. In fact, it has remained here even now.

Many Southerners moved to the North, as the growth of industrial power required a considerable number of working hands. Many stayed, and as a result, it turned out that the developed North was forced to economically support the lagging South. This didn't sit well with everyone. The Northerners, of course.

There were no significant events like large-scale protests or civil wars, but some residual tensions remained. In Italian society, friction appeared on the subject that the hardworking North is forced to support the lazy South. Not that this will prevent you from having a great time in Italy, but I would refrain from debates on this subject.

When planning your trip to Italy, keep in mind that the North is more predictable, there is more order and less chaos in the North, but it is also more expensive. In addition, Northerners are slightly more reserved, and if you need that stereotypical hot Italian hospitality that you saw in the movies, it's better to look for it in the South.

Traditional cuisine also differs depending on the region, if this is important to you (for me, for example, it's very important). Of course, traditional Sicilian "cannoli" can be tried in Milan, and it's quite possible that a Sicilian who moved to the North will prepare them for you. But it's still better to go to Sicily for Sicilian "cannoli", or at least a little further south.

But we'll come back to Italian cuisine, and most likely, more than once.

▶ *Do they speak English in Italy? Young people speak quite well, middle-aged people not so much. Therefore, if you need to clarify something with the locals, it is better to focus on young people.*

Plus, keep in mind that English is known much better in big cities than in Italian villages. So, a basic set of Italian phrases is essential there.

Some italian phrases you may need to get acquainted

Ciao, come ti chiami? [CHOW, KOH-may tee KYAH-mee?]

Hi, what's your name?

Io sono... [ee-oh SOH-noh...]

I am ... (name)

Piacere [pyah-CHAY-ray]

Nice to meet you

Di dove sei? [dee DOH-veh say?]

Where are you from?

Sono di ... [SOH-noh dee ...]

I am from ... (city or country)

Che lavoro fai? [kay lah-VOH-roh fy?]

What's your job?

Sono qui per vacanza [SOH-noh kwee pair vah-KAHN-tsah]

I'm here on vacation

Prendiamo un caffè insieme? [pren-DEE-ah-mo oon kah-FEH een-SYAY-may?]

Shall we have coffee together?

—

Chapter 3

Transport

To go in search of Sicilian cannoli or anything else, you need transport, and in Italy, it's certainly available and quite unique, as you'd expect.

As for urban transport, I always choose the metro if it's available. It works more predictably than, for example, city buses, and in summer it's also cooler. The cost is usually the same. In general, it comes with numerous advantages.

By the way, if a funicular can be considered one of the types of urban transport, I would also highly recommend it. I used it only a couple of times though. Once to climb into the old town in Umbrian Orvieto, the second time in the city of Bergamo near Milan. Both times in the small funicular car, it was quite cramped, but when you look down from the mountain after arrival, a warm gratitude spreads through the muscles of your legs towards this wonderful mode of transport :)

Now, let's talk about buses. In the North, city buses run more reliably and predictably, while in the South, they can be less reliable. What's important to know: when you're waiting for a bus at a stop, it's important to signal the driver by raising your hand; otherwise, there's a risk of watching the bus sadly drive past, because it may not stop if no one is getting off.

Getting off the bus is also not that simple. If you don't want to rush past the stop where you were supposed to get off, you need to find the red button with the inscription STOP and press it when approaching your desired stop. The buttons are usually located on the handrails and sometimes next to some seats.

To know when you're nearing your stop, I suggest using Google Maps. The stops are marked with white dots, so you'll be able to see in advance when your stop is coming up.

It's also worth keeping in mind one not-so-obvious aspect: if you plan to navigate a hilly city, a regular bus ride can become a real challenge because Italian buses navigate turns quite quickly. This can be an issue for people who are prone to motion sickness, like my younger son, for example. The problem is exacerbated during hot weather, so keep that in mind and buy motion sickness tablets in advance if needed.

If you don't plan to use city buses, you can rent a bicycle (this option is not available everywhere) or an electric scooter (also not available everywhere). Mostly, you can do this in larger cities. In the book's appendix, you'll find links to the main apps where you can do this.

It's also quite evident that you can rent a car. The bigger the car, the more expensive it is. The closer it is to the summer season, the more expensive it is. Both of these are fairly predictable and don't require additional comments, I believe.

For moving between cities, I consider the train to be the most convenient transport. Here's why:

First of all — it's not that hot on Italian trains. With very rare exceptions. If the exception has caught up with you, try moving to another carriage — it may turn out that you were riding with a non-working air conditioner for 4 hours completely in vain.

Secondly — it's not crowded, and nothing goes numb. I've been planning to buy one of those neck pillows to sleep in transport for years. I still haven't bought one because there's no need for it on the train.

Thirdly — they don't induce motion sickness. If this is relevant for you, it may turn out to be a big plus.

The fourth point is not the most obvious but equally important: it is easy to find the railway station. Even in places where you've never been before.

In any city, except for the largest ones (and there are very, very few of those in Italy), there's only one railway station. This is unlike bus stops, which can easily turn your journey from point A to point B into a fascinating quest with an unpredictable outcome.

You will be able to reach many of the places you want to visit in Italy by train. But not all routes will be direct, without transfers. More often the opposite: there will be transfers, and sometimes more than one. Therefore, pay attention to the duration of the transfer time.

A transfer time of 5-7 minutes may seem attractive to you. Great, you'll manage to get there, almost without wasting time on transfers. Super, right? But that's not always the case.

Firstly, Italian trains are very often late, and you can easily miss the train you were supposed to transfer to.

Secondly, if too little time was allocated for the transfer, you may not have enough time to figure out from which platform your train is leaving and where exactly you need to run right now. You can't just cross from one track to another; often, you need to use the passages under the tracks. This requires time, and doing it with a heavy suitcase is a dubious pleasure. Sometimes, there is an opportunity to use an elevator, which is not always available or functional.

Speaking of a comfortable transfer time, I would suggest aiming for tickets with a transfer time of around 20-25 minutes. This still doesn't guarantee that the transfer will happen on time (trains in Italy can be delayed by up to an hour), but it provides a reasonably good chance of reaching your destination comfortably and on time.

Buying a train ticket is easy, you can do it online or use a ticket vending machine at the station. Sometimes, tickets are sold at the station's bar.

An important note: if you decide to buy a ticket offline, don't forget to validate it. Otherwise, your ticket will be considered invalid, and you risk getting a fine. There are special machines on the train platform for ticket validation. They look similar to the ones you find on buses, so you're unlikely to confuse them with anything else.

What may not be obvious is that simply inserting the ticket into the designated slot is not enough. You also need to slide it to the left until it stops; otherwise, the machine won't work. It also seems important which side of the ticket you insert, but in practice, it doesn't matter much; the machine will still work, and the ticket will be considered validated.

Point your phone's camera at the QR code, and you'll be able to see how to do it.

(!) The link leads to a video, so if you have limited internet data, it's better to do this when you find the nearest Wi-Fi

If you ever consider not buying a ticket and riding without one, it's not a good idea. You'll encounter ticket controllers on the trains frequently, so riding without a ticket is not the best idea. Fines in Italy, to put it mildly, are not very lenient, so let's just forget about the possibility of traveling without a ticket.

What can indeed be considered a good idea is purchasing tickets online, for several reasons:

First of all — you don't have to stand in a queue. Imagine this: your train is departing soon, and in front of you is a line of tourists aclumsily trying to defeat the unfriendly interface of Italian ticket vending machines. One attempt, then another... The card didn't work for some reason; you need to try another... Or maybe change the language, huh?...

In general, the procedure is not for the faint of heart.

Second of all — you don't need to validate the ticket.

Imagine: your train is about to depart very soon, and you still need to validate the ticket. You have a big suitcase. No, make that two suitcases... and a child. No, make that two children. And the ticket validator is nowhere in sight. Well, it must be somewhere on the platform. But it's unclear where.

If you haven't fully grasped the horror of the situation, imagine that it's the end of July, around 3-4 pm when the platform is scorching hot like a frying pan, and the air temperature is around 38-39 degrees Celsius. Well, or 100-102 degrees Fahrenheit, even better. Can you imagine it? Great.

All of this was necessary to convince you to buy tickets online and avoid senseless adventures. You can purchase tickets directly on the Italian railway website or download the app. Either the official Italian railway app or one of the other apps that allow you to do so.

Point your phone's camera to go
to the Italian railways website:

You can download the app here
if you have an iPhone:

And here if you have an Android
phone:

The ticket will not have information about the track from which your train will depart, it must be looked for on the electronic boards. The delay time is also displayed there, if the train is late.

Also, keep in mind that if you find your platform on the departure board, it doesn't mean that the train will actually depart from there. The track can be changed a few minutes before departure, so the period before the train departs is not a time to relax. You'll have time to do that on the train, as they are quite comfortable in Italy. Right now, you should be attentive and listen to announcements over the loudspeakers. If you don't speak Italian, it's not a problem as they are always announced in English as well.

There are also taxis, but I hardly ever use them. There's one simple reason why: taxis in Italy are ruthlessly expensive. They say it's because the licenses issued by the Italian government for these types of activity are very expensive. I've even heard that these licenses are almost passed down by inheritance. I don't know how true that is, but the fact that the taxi prices are outrageously high is definitely true.

▶ *On the website of the Italian railways, you can check in real time whether your train is late. To do this, use the qr code below: open the page and enter your train number in the search (it is indicated on the ticket). After that, check if there is an ominous word "ritardo" (that is, "delay") next to your route. For example, ritardo di 15 min means "15 minute delay".*

► *On the website of the Italian railways, you can check in real time whether your train is late. To do this, use the qr code below: open the page and enter your train number in the search (it is indicated on the ticket). After that, check if there is an ominous word "ritardo" (that is, "delay") next to your route. For example, ritardo di 15 min means "15 minute delay".*

► *Be careful with night flights. The fact is that there is no night transfer in almost all airports in Italy, which means that the only way to get to the hotel will be by taxi. In most cases, the first bus or train connecting the airport with the city leaves at 5 am, and the last one at midnight. Therefore, if there is such an opportunity, book daytime flights.*

► *Not so long ago, regional train tickets purchased online became subject to mandatory check-in. It's easy to do: just click on the red button in the email you received after the purchase, select your ticket from the list, and click "Check In." You can do this on the day of travel before (!) the train departs. Without check-in, the ticket is considered invalid, so don't forget to do it.*

► *A bus ticket in Italy is bought in a rather unexpected place - in a tobacco shop, which is called "Tabaccheria". You can see a huge letter T on the sign — that's where you need to go. Keep in mind: most often they are closed on Sundays, so it is worth taking care of buying tickets in advance, if possible. They can also be sold in newspaper kiosks (in Italian "edicola"), well, at the station / bus station. In large cities, you will also see ticket vending machines, which will be the most convenient way to get them.*

In theory, you can buy a ticket from the bus driver, but I wouldn't recommend relying on it: they are often unavailable.

► *Examples of how much a taxi can cost:*

From Santa Maria Novella station to Campo Marte in Florence: 12 euros (approx. 4 km)

From the airport to the port in Genoa: 25 euros (approx. 6 km)

From Fiumicino airport to the center of Rome: 48 euros (approx. 30 km)

From the town of Amalfi to the town of Positano: 90 euros (approx. 17 km)

Some Italian phrases you may need to get around

Vorrei un biglietto per... [voh-RAY oon bee-LYET-toh pair...] I would like a ticket to... (a city)

Un biglietto di andata e ritorno, grazie [oon bee-LYET-toh dee ahn-DAH-tah eh ree-TOR-noh, GRAH-tsee-eh] A round-trip ticket, thank you

Un biglietto di sola andata, per favore [oon bee-LYET-toh dee SOH-lah ahn-DAH-tah, pair fah-VOH-ray] A one-way ticket, please

Quanto costa il biglietto? [KWAN-toh KOH-stah eel bee-LYET-toh?] How much does the ticket cost?

Quando parte il treno / l'autobus? [KWAHN-doh PAHR-teh eel TRAY-noh / LAU-toh-boos?] When does the train / bus depart?

Qual è la prossima fermata? [kwahl eh lah PROH-see-mah fair-MAH-tah?] What is the next stop?

Ci sono cambi? [chee SOH-noh KAHM-bee?] Are there any transfers?

Vorrei un taxi [voh-RAY oon TAK-se] I would like a taxi

—

Chapter 4

Climate

I live in the very center of Italy, not in the south or the north, which I believe is quite indicative for a chapter titled «Climate».

By the way, why I live in the very center of Italy is a separate and rather interesting story. I won't go into all the details since this is not a memoir but rather a manual with a modest claim to usefulness. However, this brief introduction will help you better understand what you should pay attention to.

When I moved to Italy, I didn't know where my new Italian home would be. At the same time, there were pandemic-related restrictions that complicated travel. I couldn't just go to the south, then come back and head north. So, I came up with nothing better than pointing my finger at the very center of the map and flying there. The plan was to strategically position myself in the central location and explore both the south and the north from there.

Following the established plan, I traveled all over Italy until I realized that it made absolutely no sense except for expanding my horizons, and everything I needed, I had already found. That is, I decided to stay in the very place on the map where I poked my finger in the beginning. It's funny, I agree.

But it wasn't always funny. When I first arrived, on that same evening, I decided to run away from there, and I learned a beautiful but new word for me: "Tramontana".

"Tramontana" is not a new model of Ferrari, and it's not a type of black Umbrian grape, as it might seem. It's a soul-chilling (as well as hands, feet, and other body parts) wind. Cold, darn it, just unbelievably cold... that was the last thing I expected to encounter in Italy in March.

Later, fortunately, I found out that "Tramontana" doesn't blow all the time, and overall, the climate here isn't so bad that I had to pack my bags urgently.

What is this story for? I had absolutely no idea what awaited me. The formula **{Italy + spring = okay, T-shirts will be enough}** turned out to be completely inapplicable to reality. I definitely should have prepared better.

Yes, perhaps this does not threaten you, and you are not going to Umbria. Maybe you're planning to go to a warm island. Sicily, for instance.

But even there, a surprise may await you: for example, the dusty Scirocco wind which originates in the African deserts in the African deserts and brings unbearable heat and even sandstorms to Sicily. It may catch you in March or November.

If you're not a fan of wind, you might want to skip Italy in March, as you've probably noticed. It's pretty windy in many parts at this time of year.

Of course, these are quite rare instances, but they are worth being aware of. Besides them, there are a couple of natural phenomena to pay attention to. For example, earthquakes. I experienced three of them. The first one had a magnitude of 5.7 and occurred around 7 in the morning. I didn't feel that earthquake because I was still asleep.

But the second one happened during the day, and despite its lower magnitude, it felt much more unpleasant. There was a pot of water in the kitchen sink, and when the water started splashing from side to side, it was quite unsettling.

By evening, of that same day, there was a third one. An earthquake that demonstrated how a vase can move on its own across the table which prompted me to rush outside barefoot, in an attempt to follow the safety instructions.

Speaking of instructions, here's a brief summary: if you can make it outside, do so; if not, hide under a table — it can protect you from falling debris. Alternatively, seek shelter in doorways — external walls are sturdier.

I never thought I'd be writing such a text, but in earthquake-prone areas, it's unfortunately not uncommon. There's no need to panic, but knowing what to do is important.

Summer in Italy is usually very warm, in some places turning into hot weather, and in some areas, it can get extremely hot. Last summer, the highest temperature I personally experienced was +42 degrees Celsius (108 degrees Fahrenheit). It's the kind of situation where the cold wind "Tramontana" no longer seems like a curse but becomes a wonderful gift. It's hot in June, July, and August, and sometimes even in May and September.

August is definitely a month that deserves to be mentioned because it's a unique period for Italy. If you want to go to Italy in August, it can be both a great idea and not so much. It can be great only if you are ready to pay a lot. First of all, this applies to the cost of living in hotels and apartments. Everything else, if it becomes more expensive, it is not so noticeable.

The thing is, in August, Italy celebrates "Ferragosto" or "Ferie di agosto", which are the August holidays. Technically, they last for two weeks, one week before August 15th and one week after. In reality, the entire month of August feels like a continuous holiday.

What does this mean for you:
If we are talking about tourist cities — hotels, B&Bs, apartments, rooms, campsites — everything rises sharply in price. If we are talking about seaside towns, it will be even worse.

Moreover, there's no guarantee you'll find anything even available, even if you're willing to pay more.

In coastal towns during this period, everything will be open, but in cities farther from the sea, you might often see a sign that says "Chiuso per ferie", meaning "Closed for holidays", instead of "Aperto" — which means "Open". This isn't always convenient, as you can imagine.

► *When can you swim in the sea in Italy?*
The ideal time is the months from June to August.
But in the very south of Italy (for example, in Sicily),
the swimming season lasts even longer: from May
to October. Counting on swimming in winter,
as in the Maldives, is definitely not worth it.

► *According to statistics, the rainiest months in Italy*
are October, November and December. So don't forget
an umbrella if you're planning a trip at this time.
It usually rains the least in July.

► *If you're not great with heat, I wouldn't suggest*
going to Italy in July or August. It can stay
around +35°C, or even hotter in the south. It can be
exhausting, especially if you're interested in sightseeing,
enjoying beautiful nature, and trying delicious food
rather than just relaxing on the beach. You can easily
do all of this in the spring or fall.

Some Italian phrases you may need to discuss the weather

Ho troppo freddo / caldo [oh TROP-poh
FRED-doh / KAL-doh] I'm very cold / hot

Come si accende l'aria condizionata?
[KOH-may see ah-CHEN-day L'AH-ree-ah kohn-dee-zyoh-
NAH-tah?] How do I turn on the air conditioner?

Posso accendere il riscaldamento?
[PAW-soh ah-CHEN-day eel ree-skal-dah-MEN-toh?]
Can I turn on the heating?

Come si cambia la temperatura sul termostato? [KOH-may see KAHM-byah lah tem-peh-
rah-TOO-rah sool ter-MOHS-tah-toh?]
How do I change the thermostat temperature?

Come posso abbassare la temperatura? [KOH-may PAW-soh ahb-bah-
SAH-ray lah tem-peh-rah-TOO-rah?]
How can I lower the temperature?

Il radiatore non funziona [eel rah-dee-ah-
TOH-ray nohn foon-TSYOH-nah] The radiator is not working

Che tempo fa oggi? [kay TEM-poh fah OH-jee]
What's the weather like today?

—

Chapter 5

Hotel

When it comes to temporary accommodation in Italy, it's important to plan ahead. The closer you get to the summer season (especially in August, as you already know), the harder it becomes to find suitable options.

Since this topic is quite straightforward and doesn't require a deep dive, this chapter will be short. Let's get to the point.

Where to search: I wouldn't recommend experimenting, and I would use one of the two well-known platforms: Booking or Airbnb. For a short term, it is more profitable to look on Booking, and for a period of more than 5-7 days on Airbnb.

What you should pay attention to: it's important to review the cancellation policies in case something goes wrong with your booking. Most hosts in Italy now offer free cancellation up until the date of arrival. I would recommend not passing up this option. You should also carefully read the rental conditions.

In most cases, everything will be fine since Italians generally know how to host guests well. But there are still a few things you should know about.

There are some non-traditional ways of renting accommodation that you might encounter. For example, the host might not include bed linens and towels in the rental price and charge an additional fee for them. That is, you find a house that suits you in price, and then it turns out that it is actually much more expensive than others because of these extra charges. You probably won't want to bring towels and bed linens with you.

Breakfast is often included, and it's usually a bit of a mystery. Sometimes it might consist of a couple of dry biscuits with jam, while other times, it could be a luxurious spread with fresh pastries and poached eggs. It's hard to tell as apartment descriptions typically don't specify breakfast details. However, you can often find more information about this in reviews.

You might also unexpectedly discover that your room is private, but the bathroom is shared. This means you'll be sharing it with other guests. Or the bathroom could be private, but you have to walk through a common corridor to access it. Not the most pleasant experience, as you can imagine. Therefore, read the description carefully.

It's often mentioned in the description that there's a kitchen. If you're renting an apartment, these usually come at a higher price. However, the quality of the kitchen can vary significantly. Keep in mind that sometimes a "kitchen" might consist of just a couple of cabinets and an electric kettle. Additionally, some basic essentials may be missing from the kitchen, like salt and pepper.

Conversely, some places might provide plenty of amenities like salt, coffee, tea, sugar, and olive oil. So it's better to clarify with the host what exactly this kitchen is like.

Besides the room rate, there is a city tourist tax to consider. It's often not included in the room rate and can range from 1 to 5 euros per person per night. Many hosts ask for the city tax to be paid in cash, so it's a good idea to have a few coins on hand when you check in.

During check-in, the host will likely ask for your permission to make a copy of your documents, as they are required by law to notify the immigration police of your check-in. This is just a formality and shouldn't concern you.

Also, pay attention to the check-in and check-out times, especially the check-out time. It's common for checkout to be as early as 10 am, while your train might not depart until the evening. In such cases, it's a good idea to try to arrange with the host to store your luggage ahead of time because otherwise, you'd be wasting a whole day in a new, potentially very interesting city. Sometimes hosts may offer a slightly later check-out, but this is not very common. Apartments in Italy are usually occupied, especially during the high season.

▶ *How much does it cost to rent a room for two in Italy? If it is a large city like Rome or Florence, expect to pay around 100-120 euros per night. For this amount, you will get a classic hotel with no unpleasant or pleasant surprises. In smaller cities, a night in a hotel will cost around 80 euros.*

However, don't forget that everything is more expensive in the north of Italy (so it's better to add 20 percent to the price just in case) and cheaper in the south (here you can subtract 20%).

And I will also remind you about Ferragosto: most often, 150 euros per night is the minimum you can expect to pay in August on the coast.

▶ *If your trip falls in summer, especially in August, book your accommodation as early as possible. The best options for the end of summer will already be booked by early April.*

But if you missed the opportunity, do not despair: some hotels open reservations shortly before the arrival date, so it makes sense to check from time to time whether new options have appeared. Keep in mind that when booking at the last moment, you will most likely overpay by about 20 percent.

Some Italian phrases you may need for hotel interactions

Ho una prenotazione a nome... [oh OO-nah preh-noh-tah-TSYOH-nay ah NOH-may...]
I have a reservation under the name...

Ecco sono i miei documenti [EH-koh SOH-noh ee myay dohk-oo-MEN-tee] Here are my documents

Qual è la password del WI-FI? [kwahl eh lah PAS-werd del WAI-FAI?] What's the Wi-Fi password?

Posso avere la chiave della camera?
[PAW-soh ah-VEH-ray lah KEE-ah-vay DEL-lah KAH-meh-rah?] Can I get the key to my room?

A che ora devo lasciare la stanza? [ah kay OH-rah DEH-voh lah-SHAH-ray lah STAHN-zah?]
What time do I need to check-out?

A che ora è la colazione? [ah kay OH-rah eh lah koh-lah-TSYOH-nay?] What time is breakfast?

Vorrei fare il check-out [voh-RAY FAH-ray eel chek-OWT] I'd like to check-out

Avete il servizio navetta? [ah-VEH-tay eel ser-VEE-tsyo nah-VET-tah?] Do you have a shuttle service?

Chapter 6

Food and wine

Food in Italy is not just food; it's an essential part of Italians' lives and a universal topic for discussion with both friends and strangers.

Only in Italy, when you meet someone, they would ask, "What did you eat today?" Even at the post office, you can easily and casually discuss the recipe for proper Italian pasta with the postal workers. It's hard to imagine a prolonged conversation among Italians that doesn't involve discussions about food. Sooner or later, this topic will inevitably come up. Regardless of what was discussed before, just as all roads lead to Rome, any conversation in Italy leads to discussions about food. In short, food in Italy is almost like a religion.

And sometimes even more so, considering that Italians have a relatively relaxed attitude toward religion, despite the presence of numerous churches, religious holidays, and the close proximity to the Vatican.

Despite the fact that food in Italy is almost a religion, not all Italians are so religious if it concerns tourists, meaning you in this case. Some residents of the Italian Peninsula will easily break the Ten Commandments of Cuisine or even more if they realize you're a tourist and know nothing about it.

So, our task is not to be tourists, as strange as it may sound. Of course, we can't become experts in Italian products overnight, as there's not enough time for that, but having some basics won't hurt. Italians always choose Italian products. Partly this is correct, but only partly.

Almost any product in Italy with "Italia" written on it automatically becomes more expensive. Or rather, it's valued more highly. And this has nothing to do with the quality of the products — it's about the Italians' attitude towards their country, which I never cease to admire: "our Italian is the very best — no doubts about it." Even if you have to pay an extra twenty percent for the idea.

We don't necessarily have to pay extra for the idea, so you can decide for yourself whether to pay extra or not.

As for wine, let's be frank: not all of us are versed in wines so much that we can determine the vintage by the smell of a wine cork.Fortunately, there's an instruction manual for beginners.

Take a bottle of wine in your hand (white or red — doesn't matter) and look for the abbreviation D.O.C. on the label. This abbreviation stands for "Denominazione di origine controllata," which means that the wine's origin is controlled by special authorities and meets quality standards.

You might also come across D.O.C.G. That's even better: controlled and guaranteed. And that's it. Those aforementioned authorities have already done everything for you; all you need to do is find a bottle with the right labeling on the shelf.

If you see the abbreviation DOC or DOCG without periods, don't worry; it can be written both ways. To make it easier to spot, look at the top part of the bottle where the cork is: wines in the DOC category usually have a blue paper ribbon indicating the category, while DOCG wines have a brown one.

Obtaining the D.O.C. or D.O.C.G. designation in Italy is not something that can be done easily, which effectively safeguards you from buying low-quality wine.

Although, to be honest, in Italy, you'd have to look pretty hard for that. Typically, if you're buying a bottle of wine in the mid-price range without trying to save too much, you'll be just fine.

► *Iconic Italian products to try:*

Parmigiano Reggiano — Parmesan cheese

Mozzarella di bufala — Buffalo mozzarella cheese

Pesto — Pesto sauce

Liquore Limoncello — Limoncello liqueur

Aceto balsamico —Balsamic vinegar

Prosciutto di Parma — Parma ham

Pecorino Romano — Pecorino Romano cheese

Mortadella — Mortadella sausage

Some Italian words you may need to talk about food

il pesce [eel PEH-sheh]
fish

la carne [lah KAR-neh]
meat

il pane [eel PAH-neh]
bread

la frutta [lah FROOT-tah]
fruit

la verdura [lah ver-DOO-rah]
vegetables

il formaggio [eel for-MAH-joh]
cheese

il burro [eel BOO-roh]
butter

l'aglio [LAH-lyoh]
garlic

i funghi [ee FOON-gee]
mushrooms

Chapter 7

Local market

Perhaps it's best to begin your introduction to the incredible variety of Italian products right here — at the Italian market. Often markets in Italy aren't stationary; they materialize right on the city square on specific days of the week.

Let me give you an example. I live in Umbria, in the Italian city of Perugia. Here's how it works for us: once a week, on Wednesdays, a food market sets up in the city center. On Saturdays, there's another food market in a different location, farther from the center, where everything is much cheaper. I would even say it's about half the price.

I go to the market once a week, the one in the city center. It's not so much about buying groceries as it is about a weekly ritual. After a few weeks of practicing this ritual, it became evident that there are many enthusiasts for it, and it's almost always the same people.

In the end, all of this begins to resemble something like a secret order. Every week, a group of people gather in the same place. Early in the morning while the city sleeps. Like a secret meeting of a Masonic lodge — with the only difference that its members are not at all interested in either world domination or conspiracy theories. They are interested in fresh zucchini and pleasant morning conversations about pasta recipes.
In general, I like it.

If you feel the same excitement as I do about the opportunity to run your fingertips over the rough heads of Italian artichokes and inhale deeply the sweet scent of fresh figs, you'll understand me.

If not, no worries, you won't lose anything, and you'll still buy quality products for lunch. Plus, you won't risk becoming known as the city eccentric who strokes artichokes and sniffs figs :)

By the way, usually the price for vegetables and fruits is indicated per kilogram, but sometimes it's per piece, like for avocados or artichokes, for example. Pay close attention to the price tag. If it says something like "al pezzo," "al pz," or simply "pz," that means it's the price per piece, not per kilogram.

If you forget something, you can buy it at small family-owned shops. There are usually many of them in any Italian city. They don't operate like the market, on specific days, but rather every day except Sunday. They typically have a "pausa pranzo," so keep this in mind. "Pausa pranzo" translates to lunch break, and it's somewhat similar to the Spanish siesta, with post-lunch hours of rest. Around 1 PM, these shops close and reopen later in the evening, usually around 4 PM. This applies not only to grocery stores but to all other shops in Italy except for large chain stores and shops catering to tourists. But you have nothing to do there, so let's focus on the authentic Italian stores that have been practicing "pausa pranzo" for decades.

Prices at small family-owned shops are usually quite high, but they have a special charm that, in my opinion, is worth the price difference, even if it's sometimes significant.

The other day, I bought vegetables at the market and realized on my way home that I had completely forgotten about parsley. I had plans to make "puttanesca" pasta for dinner, no way without parsley.

I decided it would be easier to pop into a small vegetable shop:

— Good evening, what can I get you?

— A bunch of parsley, please.

— Anything else?

— No, thank you, I have everything; I just forgot to buy parsley. How much do I owe you?

— Nothing; it's just parsley.

It was the feeling of bringing home something much more valuable than just a bunch of parsley. It's amazing how simple it can be. And it's not about money. It's not even about the parsley.

▶ *By the way, keep in mind that it is not very*
common to bargain at Italian markets.
Usually, everyone pays the price that the seller quotes.

▶ *Sometimes a market is just a market.*
And sometimes it's a whole performance. I'm talking
about southern Italian cities like Palermo or Naples.
It's so noisy there that you risk not hearing your own
voice: sellers shout at the top of their lungs, praising
their goods and convincing you to buy The Most
Delicious Tomatoes in the World from them.

Not everyone will like it, but the experience
is definitely interesting.

Some Italian phrases you may need for market conversations

Quanto costa al chilo? [KWAN-toh KOH-stah ahl KEE-loh?] How much does it cost per kilogram? (1 kg ≈ 2.2 lbs)

Vorrei un etto / mezzo chilo / un chilo / un litro di... [voh-RAY oon EH-toh / MED-dzoh KEE-loh / oon KEE-loh / oon LEE-troh dee...] I would like 100 grams / half a kilo / a kilo / a liter of ...

Posso avere un po' di...? [PAW-soh ah-VEH-ray oon poh dee...?] Can I have a little bit of...?

Potrei avere un assaggio? [poh-TRAY ah-VEH-ray oon ah-SAH-joh?] Can I try it?

Che cos'è questo? [kay koz-EH KWEH-stoh?] What is this?

Da dove viene? [dah DOH-veh VYEH-neh?] Where is it from?

E' fresco? [ay FRES-koh?] Is it fresh?

Quanto viene in tutto? [KWAN-toh VYEH-neh in TOO-toh?] How much will it be in total?

Chapter 8

Supermarket

If Italian markets don't appeal to you or you want to save a bit, a supermarket is a good idea. As you already know, food is a cult in Italy, and this is strictly followed not only by family shops but also by large supermarket chains. So, as a rule, everything will be fresh and quite appetizing, and there should be no unpleasant surprises.

Here's what you need to know about it. Inside the supermarket there are departments where there is a separate queue, even before the queue at the checkout. Usually, this is the section where they sell bread and pastries, as well as the section where they slice "mortadella", "salami", and delicious "prosciutto" — Italian ham. It's important not to forget to take a number. Look for an electronic display or a round plastic device with a paper strip — it can be either one or the other. In the supermarket where I shop, they have both. The one where they sell bread uses an analog paper system, while the one for "prosciutto" and "mortadella" uses a digital display.

In the department with vegetables and fruits, you'll need to weigh your purchases yourself. When weighing, make sure to enter the product number, which is usually displayed next to the price. It's important not to forget this number while heading to the scales. The scales may not always be nearby. I, for example, often forget.

Just like at the market, you may come across the abbreviation "al pz" or simply "pz." This means you don't need to weigh the product; it's priced per piece, not per kilogram. If it's packaged in a tray, then the price is for the entire tray.

I can't offer specific recommendations on choosing products as it's a matter of personal taste, but I can tell you what to look out for in Italy. So here's my list:

• Incredibly fragrant **Italian basil** in pots

• **Peperone** — sweet bell peppers (especially in summer season)

• **Roman salad**

• **Lemons** (it's better to buy those sold per piece rather than by weight; they might be slightly more expensive, but they're better)

• **Tuna in cans** (I'll tell you what to do with it a bit later)

• Fresh **mozzarella cheese**

• **Italian pasta**

• **Canned tomatoes** (in Italian, it should say "pomodori pelati" on the can)

- **Anchovies**

- **Marinated olives** (better to buy them by weight, not in jars)

- Crusty Italian bread **"Ciabatta"**

- **Olive oil** (make sure it's cold-pressed, and the bottle should say "extra vergine")

- **Garlic**

- **Fresh parsley** (we'll need this later too)

- **Capers** (we'll need them later as well)

And don't forget to buy a bottle of Italian **"Chinotto."** It's a fizzy drink made from almost black oranges. Very interesting taste, give it a try.

Well, that's about it. By the way, not too long ago, in Italy there were problems with card payment from time to time. Now this is rather an exception, cards are accepted everywhere. However, it's still a good idea to have some cash with you.

Once, I went to the supermarket, waited my turn at the checkout, packed my groceries into bags, and then the cashier informed me that they were having internet issues, so they couldn't accept cards today. I didn't have any cash with me. It resulted in a rather silly situation: walking away after packing a whole bag of groceries is strange, and yet you can't pay for your purchase. In the end, I had to ask the cashier to hold onto the items, go back home to get cash, and then return to pay for the groceries. It's funny, but when I returned, card payments were already working again.

Now that you've returned home with bags full of luxurious Italian groceries, let's prepare some real pasta. Something not too complicated, like pasta with tuna.

So, here's what you'll need:

....

- **Pasta** (Italians often use "rigatoni") — 400 g

- **Tuna** —280 g

- **Whole peeled tomatoes in a can** — 500 g

- **Garlic** — 2 or 3 cloves

- **Olives** — 70 g

- **Capers** — about one teaspoon

- **Extra virgin olive oil**

- **A bit of parsley**

- **Water**

- **Salt**

....

Here's how to cook it:

Start by bringing a pot of water to a boil. Salt the water (I use a full tablespoon for a large pot). When the water boils, add the pasta. The package will indicate how many minutes to cook it. It's very important to leave it "al dente," so I recommend setting a timer on your phone to make sure you don't miss the right moment.

While that's heating up, warm some extra virgin olive oil in a wide pan. Into the oil, add 2-3 cloves of garlic, thinly sliced (if they are large, use 2; if they are small, use 3). Alternatively, you can crush the garlic cloves with the back of a knife if you prefer to remove it later. I usually leave it, so I slice it. Don't let it brown too much; as soon as it becomes golden, add the tomatoes. You can chop the tomatoes with a knife beforehand. After adding the tomatoes, let them cook in their juices.

Throw in olives, and about 5-6 minutes before the pasta is ready, add the tuna. After that, add a bit of pasta water using a ladle or a cup (I do it with a cup, I'll explain why later) and mix everything well. A couple of minutes later, add the capers. About a minute before the pasta is cooked, stir in the finely chopped parsley. Drain the pasta through a colander and transfer it to the pan with the sauce. Mix it well, and you're done. Enjoy your delicious pasta with tuna!

Oh, right, I promised to explain about the cup. This cup is my personal life hack for making authentic Italian pasta. It's the most important tool after the wide skillet to ensure perfect pasta.

So, with this cup, you should scoop out some water from the pot where the pasta is boiling, right before draining it. Then, set the cup aside, as you'll need it later. This water has a lot of starch, which is great for the sauce. It's better to scoop water from the top, the frothy part.

So, when you have this cup, you can always add a bit of liquid to your sauce if the pasta turns out a bit dry. But only add it if it's really necessary. Mi raccomando — pay attention, that is.

After adding the water, vigorously mix the pasta. This will release even more starch and give you a sauce, not a soup.

Enjoy your delicious pasta with tuna, and don't hesitate to garnish it with a touch of parsley.

Buon appetito!

▶ *24-hour supermarkets are not common in Italy.*
They are usually open until 8 p.m., and many
are completely closed on Sundays.
What does this mean for you? If you arrive
in a new city on a Sunday or late in the evening,
think about snacks in advance so you don't
end up hungry.

▶ *The most popular supermarket chains are:*
Conad, COOP, Lidl, Carrefour, Pam,
Esselunga, Aldi, Prix

Some Italian phrases you may need for supermarket shopping

Dov'è il supermercato più vicino? [doh-VEH eel soo-per-mer-CAH-toh pyoo vee-CHEE-noh?]

Where is the nearest supermarket?

Dove posso trovare ... ? [DOH-veh PAW-soh troh-VAH-ray ... ?] Where can I find ... ? (a product)

Dove posso prendere il carrello? [DOH-veh PAW-soh PREHN-deh-ray eel kar-REL-loh?]

Where can I take a cart?

Posso avere un pezzo di ... ? [PAW-soh ah-VEH-ray oon PET-tsoh dee ... ?] Can I have a piece of ... (product)?

Basta così, grazie [BAHS-tah koh-ZEE, GRAH-tsee-eh] That's enough, thank you

Posso avere una busta? [PAW-soh ah-VEH-ray OO-nah BOOS-tah?] Can I have a bag?

Vorrei pagare con carta [voh-RAY pah-GAH-ray kohn KAR-tah] I would like to pay by card

Vorrei pagare in contanti [voh-RAY pah-GAH-ray in kon-TAHN-tee] I would like to pay in cash

—

Chapter 9

Restaurant

If you don't want to cook pasta yourself, you can have it prepared for you in a restaurant, usually for around 14-16 euros. Of course, this is just an average price, and it can be lower or significantly higher depending on the type of restaurant, ingredients used, the generosity of the owner, and the mood of the chef (the last part is a joke, of course.)

In Italy, dishes are typically served one after another, so it's important to understand the order in which they come. Usually, the items on the menu follow a specific sequence, with the exception of beverages, which are often found on the last pages of the menu. The wine list is often presented separately.

By the way, before the pandemic, Italy didn't have QR code menus, but after it ended, some establishments preferred not to change anything, and instead of a physical menu, they may provide you with a card containing a QR code. So leaving your phone in the room with the intention of having a digital detox might not be the best idea. I speak from experience; I tried it. After realizing I didn't have my phone with me, I had to listen carefully to the list of dishes, trying to remember something. In general, I didn't like it, so I don't recommend doing that.

Sometimes, there may not be a menu at all. They simply tell you, "Today we have such-and-such dishes for lunch." There are some choices, but they're often quite limited. This is typically practiced by small family restaurants. I like such places because the food is delicious, and the prices are reasonable.

After you've settled at your table and received the menu, the waiter will ask you what you'd like to drink. While you're perusing the menu and making your choices, your drinks will already be brought to you.

So, what comes after what:

- **Antipasto** (appetizer)

- **Primo piatto** (first course)

- **Secondo piatto** (second course)

- **Dolce** (dessert)

By default, the dishes will be brought to you in this sequence, so if you have different preferences, it's better to inform your waiter in advance.

It's a common practice in Italy for the waiter to open the wine bottle at your table and ask who will taste the wine. Afterward, the chosen volunteer will taste a small amount of the wine from the just-opened bottle. I won't pretend to be a sommelier and explain how to swirl the wine in the glass to reveal all the notes mentioned on the label, as I don't understand much about it. So, if I'm the chosen one, I happily sip the wine and inform the waiter that it's excellent. I'm not sure what would happen if one were to respond that the wine isn't very good, as I've never tried doing that. Neither have most Italians, as far as I know.

When it comes to Italian cuisine, it's too diverse to give specific recommendations for dish choices, so there won't be a long list of recommendations. Instead, there's just one single point:

Order dishes from the local cuisine.

Yes, I understand. Sometimes you might crave fish or seafood. Sometimes you might want a big grilled beef steak or something else. But in Italy, it doesn't work that way.

I live in the Umbria region, which is about 100 kilometers from the sea, or maybe a little more. But by Italian standards, the sea is almost on another continent. Every time, without a single exception, when I attempted to order seafood in local establishments, they were, at best, just edible. However, if you drive those 100 kilometers towards the sea, the situation will dramatically change for the better.

Although it's very likely that in that case, the steak might suffer. In other words, the fish will be excellent, but the meat won't be. Or the mushrooms. Or something else. In short, I think you get the idea.

The last thing I want to add to the chapter about Italian restaurants is that you will most likely find an item on the bill called "coperto." Sometimes it also appears under the name "servizio". This is a fee for service, tablecloths, utensils, and so on. Usually, it is around 1.5-2 euros per person. It can be a bit more, but I've never seen it exceed 3 euros. In this case, you don't need to leave a tip — you've already paid for it.

However, there are some exceptions. In one Roman restaurant I sometimes go to, they have a "coperto" fee, but the waiter informs you that it doesn't include the service, subtly hinting that it wouldn't hurt to leave a little tip.

▶ *As soon as you sit down at the table, the waiter will offer you a bottle of water (still or sparkling). Later, it will be included in the bill as a separate item (usually about 2 euros). If you don't need it, you can decline. They will also put a basket of bread or focaccia on the table. But you don't have to pay extra for it; bread is already included in the coperto.*

▶ *How much does what cost? (Prices are indicated for a typical Italian restaurant not overlooking the Colosseum — keep this in mind.)*

Pasta: 11-13 euros
Main course of meat or fish: 16-20 euros
Side dish: 5 euros
Dessert: 5-7 euros

▶ *I can't give you recommendations on what to try in all Italian cities (as you understand, there are too many of them), but I can suggest a few dishes from Roman cuisine, since it's highly likely that you'll visit Rome on your first trip to Italy. So:*

Artichokes alla romana

Pizza with zucchini flowers and anchovies

Saltimbocca (a thin slice of veal wrapped in prosciutto crudo, seasoned with sage)

► *What you will find on the menu:*

Antipasti (appetizers) — these are usually bruschettas, meat and cheese platters, and other small treats to keep you entertained while waiting for the main courses.

Primi piatti (first courses) — this section includes pasta, a lot of different pasta. You may also find risotto, ravioli, and tortellini here.

Secondi piatti (second courses) — this is where you'll find meat or fish dishes. A side dish is usually not included and is ordered separately.

Contorni (side dishes) — in most cases, you'll find baked potatoes, french fries, and stewed vegetables.

Dolci (desserts) — this is where all kinds of sweets are offered, as you might expect.

► *How can you gauge the average price level at a restaurant you're about to enter? Take a look at the cost of tiramisu (this dessert is almost always on the menu).*

If it costs 5-6 euros, you're at a typical restaurant with standard Italian prices. A price of 7-8 euros suggests that other dishes might also be slightly above average. If tiramisu is priced at 10 euros, it's a reason to be cautious: you might be dealing with a very touristy (and possibly less scrupulous) establishment.

Some Italian phrases you may need for dining out

Vorrei prenotare un tavolo per le sette [voh-RAY preh-noh-TAH-ray oon TAH-voh-loh pair lay SEHT-teh]

I would like to book a table for seven o'clock

Avete un tavolo per due? [ah-VEH-tay oon TAH-voh-loh pair doo-eh?] Do you have a table for two?

Possiamo ordinare? [poh-SEE-ah-mohr or-dee-NAH-ray?] Can we place an order?

Qual è la vostra specialità? [kwahl eh lah VOS-trah speh-tsyah-lee-TAH?] What's your signature dish?

Cosa ci consiglia? [KOH-zah chee kohn-SEE-lyah?]

What would you recommend?

Vorrei ... [voh-RAY ...]

I would like...... (a dish)

Posso usare il bagno? [PAW-soh oo-ZAH-ray eel BAH-nyoh?] May I use the restroom?

Il conto, per favore [eel KOHN-toh, pair fah-VOH-ray] The bill, please

Tutto era buonissimo [TOOT-toh EH-rah bwaw-NEE-ssee-mo] Everything was delicious

—

Chapter 10

Pizzeria

An important thing to understand is that despite Italian pizzerias may look like restaurants, they are not quite the same.

Pizzerias are more casual, so don't expect designer interiors, snow-white starched tablecloths, or an army of highly-trained wait staff accompanied by a selection of exquisite wines. Although there are no designer interiors in many expensive Italian restaurants either. No, you'll find tables of various sizes, a variety of chairs, and tablecloths with all sorts of patterns. Often there's no polished design by the book. Personally, I really like it.

Let's get back to the Italian pizzeria: the tablecloths might very well be paper, and instead of a wine list, you'll be offered beer and "vino della casa"— house wine served by the glass decanter. You'll have a choice of two options: red or white. Simple, right?

Oh, and you can also choose the volume of the glass decanter: 1 liter, half a liter, or 250 grams. In Italy, they often use the term "un quarto," which means a quarter-liter.

By the way, in addition to the usual round pizza, you might come across pizza "al taglio", which is sold by weight. It's typically baked on large rectangular trays, and you can choose a slice of any size. In such places, there might not even be tables — you grab your slice and go enjoy it in the park or on a nearby bench, admiring the splendid Italian views.

However, all of the above doesn't mean that giving up a restaurant in favor of an Italian pizzeria is a bad idea. If you choose the right place, you'll be treated to a simple but incredibly delicious pizza made from the freshest ingredients. Take note that Italian pizzas are divided into two main categories:

Pizze bianche: pizzas without tomato sauce.

Pizze rosse: pizzas with tomato sauce.

Although some time ago, Italian pizzerias started offering a separate category of pizza called "Pizza Gourmet." Usually, you can find such pizzas in a separate section of the menu with headings like "Pizze Gourmet," "Pizze particolari," or "Pizze speciali." Of course, the headings can be more imaginative, but the essence is that they offer a non-traditional Italian pizza recipe, but something more unusual. At times, it can even resemble a culinary experiment — sometimes quite successful, and sometimes not so much.

When I come to a pizzeria and peruse the menu, for some reason, I always find myself going back to the list of pizzas under the heading "Pizze tradizionali" —

in other words, the regular list of traditional Italian pizzas. But the choice is ultimately yours.

One thing you should definitely not ignore is the Italian phrase "Forno a legna." In fact, you should actively seek this out because seeing this phrase means that the pizzeria has a genuine wood-fired oven, which undoubtedly enhances any pizza, whether it's a traditional one or a bold culinary experiment.

By the way, below I'll provide a small list of Italian pizzas that could be considered traditional. It's clear that there's no final version of such a list, but it will serve as a guide and help you make a choice. So, here's what I usually look for on the menu.

Pizza Marinara

One of the simplest pizzas with garlic, olive oil, and incredible Italian tomato sauce. Well, a little oregano for aroma. There's not even any cheese. And you absolutely don't want to add it — everything is already perfect as it is.

Pizza Margherita

This pizza is named after Queen Margherita, which, as many believe, was created by the Neapolitan Raffaele Esposito in 1889. Although Italians are not unanimous on this matter and have been engaged in long standing disputes about whether this is true.

I rarely order this pizza, but my younger son loves it. And he's very picky about food. So that's a good sign — perhaps you'll probably like it too ;)

What's in it: tomato sauce, extra virgin olive oil, mozzarella cheese, and the most important ingredient — fresh aromatic basil leaves. Mmm... soon, it seems, I'll change my mind and join the numerous fans of this pizza.

Pizza Tonno e Cipolla
(Tuna and onions)

It's also a pretty simple pizza: tomato sauce, canned tuna, red onion, and a bit of oregano. Yes, I know how the combination "canned tuna" sounds. But just give it a try.

Pizza Quattro Formaggi
(Four cheeses)

It's all clear from the name: it contains 4 Italian cheeses. Some of them have a more delicate taste, such as mozzarella and fontina cheese, which is made using milk from the Italian region of Valle d'Aosta (the one with picturesque Alps, postcard-like meadows, and happy cows from yogurt commercials).

Plus, a couple of cheeses with a stronger flavor — grated Parmesan cheese and soft blue cheese gorgonzola. In general, it's delicious, as you already understand.

There's no need to describe all types of pizza in detail, but I just want to draw your attention to ones like Pizza Napoli, Pizza Capricciosa, Pizza Boscaiola and Pizza alla Diavola if you like it spicier.

Oh, I almost forgot my favorite Roman pizza, Pizza Fiori di Zucca e Alici. It has zucchini flowers, tender mozzarella, and salty anchovies. And it's on good dough — that's important.

By the way, when it comes to ingredients in pizza, it's usually harder to make a mistake than with the dough.

The main challenge often lies precisely in the dough. If you suddenly feel inspired and decide to make pizza yourself, you'll need a tried-and-true dough recipe. And I have such a recipe.

I've detailed the recipe, explaining what to do and how. Just follow along, and everything will turn out fine.

Point your phone's camera at the QR code, and you'll have the verified recipe for Italian pizza dough :)

► *In different regions of Italy, there are various traditions for making pizza: with thick crust, thin crust, or high edges. So, if you're served a pizza that looks different from what you're used to, don't be quick to get upset. It might be very tasty; it's just prepared a little differently in this city.*

► *How much does what cost?*

A piece of pizza al taglio — 2-3 euros

The simplest pizza (like Margherita or Marinara) whole — 7-8 euros

Classic pizza whole — 8-10 euros

► *If the Italian pizza seems too big for you to finish in one sitting, don't worry: you can always ask to have the uneaten part of the pizza boxed up to take with you. Such a request won't surprise anyone.*

Some Italian phrases you may need for ordering at a pizzeria

Una "Margherita", per favore [OO-nah MAR-geh-REE-tah, pair fah-VOH-ray]

A Margherita pizza, please

Quanto tempo ci vuole per la pizza?
[KWAN-toh TEM-poh chee VWAW-lay pair lah PEET-sah?]

How long does it take to get the pizza?

Cosa avete da bere? [KOH-zah ah-VEH-tay dah BEH-ray?] What beverages do you have?

Vorrei una birra [voh-RAY OO-nah BEER-rah]

I would like some beer

Vorrei un bicchiere di vino [voh-RAY oon bee-KYER-ray dee VEE-noh] I would like a glass of wine

Mangio qui [MAHN-joh kwee]

I will eat in here (meaning "in a pizzeria, not takeaway")

Vorrei una pizza da portar via [voh-RAY OO-nah PEET-sah dah por-TAHR VEE-ah]

I would like a pizza for takeout

Avete pizza al taglio? [ah-VEH-tay PEET-sah ahl TAH-lyoh?]

Do you have pizza by the slice?

—

Chapter 11

Bar

Did you know that ABSOLUTELY EVERY Italian word ends with a vowel? Surprisingly, it's really true. Except for words borrowed from other languages. Like the word "bar."

You could say that "bar" is just a place where you can get your morning espresso and treat yourself to a refreshing Aperol Spritz in the evening. And that's absolutely true. But in Italy, a "bar" is something entirely different.

In Italy, a bar holds far greater significance than just a place with cups and glasses. It's a meeting place for residents of nearby homes, a reading room, a smoking room, a gentlemen's club, a women's club, a place to relax, and an analog version of Tinder. Only after all of that is it a place where you can have an espresso or an Aperol Spritz.

By the way, the smoking room in an Italian bar is now more of a formality because smoking indoors has been banned in Italy for over 10 years. Since Italians are a fairly smoking-prone nation, not everyone was pleased with this change, but there are those who decided it was for the best. Italians continued to smoke a lot, but now it's done outside.

Electronic cigarette substitutes, by the way, are also not allowed to be used indoors, so keep that in mind. I've never seen anyone fined for it, but I think the bar owner will quickly ask you to move to the smoking area outside.

What else should you know about an Italian bar? Prices can vary (sometimes significantly) depending on whether you will be drinking directly at the bar counter or at a table. It's more expensive at a table, naturally.

If you want to feel a bit more like a true Italian and less like a tourist, you shouldn't order an "americano." The Americano made its way to Italy only towards the end of World War II, in 1943, when the Allies landed in the southern town of Salerno. Until that point, nobody in Italy had heard of an "americano." It got its name because American soldiers would ask to dilute the strong Italian coffee with hot water. Italians didn't see the point in this and called the new coffee "americano," referring to it among themselves as "acqua sporca" (dirty water). Not the most appealing recommendation, as you can imagine. Yes, Italians could have been more courteous to their liberators, but Italians are who they are.

When Italians say "coffee," by default they mean espresso. By the way, there's a simple test to determine whether the espresso is good: open a packet of sugar and teleport its contents confidently into your cup.

Then there are two possible outcomes: the sugar will immediately sink to the bottom of the cup like the "Titanic" or it will stay piled on top of the foam. The first outcome is bad, the second is good.

Oh, and in Italy, they usuall order "cappuccino" only until 12 pm. Why? I don't know. I've asked Italian friends many times what's wrong with having a "cappuccino" at 3, 4, 5 pm and beyond, but there's no clear answer. Well, let's just know that it's the way it is.

▶ *How much does what cost?*

Espresso — 1.20 euros

Cappuccino — 1.50 euros

Croissant — 1.50 euros

Freshly squeezed orange juice — 3 euros

Ice cream — 2 scoops for 2.5 euros

Beer 0.3 l — 5 euros

Glass of wine — 5-7 euros

Aperol Spritz — 5 euros

► *The price of coffee in an Italian bar isn't always the same. A cup of espresso that you drink at the bar counter will be cheaper than one served to you at a table. In most cases, the difference will be about 1 euro.*

► *Drinking coffee with a view of the Pantheon in Rome or the Grand Canal in Venice may not be the best idea. Often, prices there are not just 2, but 3-5 times higher than usual. At the same time, the croissant might be slightly stale, and the coffee not the best.*

However, this doesn't mean you should never choose bars near attractions. If your goal is to enjoy the atmosphere and vivid impressions, it might still be worth it.

► *By the way, as a tourist, a bar can be an extremely useful place for you. Firstly, in larger bars, you can ask for the Wi-Fi password. Secondly, in any bar, you can use the restroom—just purchase at least a symbolic cup of espresso. Sometimes you can ask to use the restroom even if you haven't bought anything, but it's more polite to still get a coffee, a bottle of water, or something similar.*

Some Italian phrases you may need to hang out at a bar

Vorrei un caffè, grazie [voh-RAY oon kah-FEH, GRAH-tsee-eh] I would like some coffee, thank you

Due cappuccini, per favore [doo-eh kahp-poo-CHEE-nee, pair fah-VOH-ray] Two cappuccinos, please

Un bicchiere d'acqua naturale, per favore [oon bee-KYER-ray DAH-kwah nah-too-RAH-lay, pair fah-VOH-ray] A glass of still water, please

Che tipi di cornetti avete? [kay TEE-pee dee kor-NET-tee ah-VEH-tay?] What types of croissants do you have?

Ci sono i cornetti al cioccolato? [chee SOH-noh ee kor-NET-tee ahl choh-koh-LAH-toh?] Do you have croissants with chocolate filling?

Vorrei qualcosa di dolce / salato [voh-RAY kwahl-KOH-zah dee DOHL-chay / sah-LAH-toh] I would like something sweet / savory

Vorrei una bevanda alcolica / analcolica [voh-RAY OO-nah beh-VAHN-dah al-KOH-lee-kah / ah-nahl-KOH-lee-kah] I'd like an alcoholic / non-alcoholic drink

—

Chapter 12

The Italians

Most likely, you have already read the previous 11 chapters, packed your swimsuit and straw hat in a suitcase, and checked if you have enough spare memory cards for your camera. Take a few more — photos of Italy look fantastic, so they will definitely not be excessive. Ready? Great.

The previous 11 chapters had a lot of useful advice, life hacks, glossaries, and ways to organize your stay in Italy optimally and correctly. Each of the 11 chapters will be useful to you in their own way. But this 12th chapter is more important than all 11 combined.

Despite the fact that Italy, as we have already found out, looks great in photos, that's not the most important thing. It's not what will make your First Time in Italy unforgettable. But it definitely will. And the reason your journey will be unforgettable is not the beauty of the country or the food, but the Italians themselves.

They will make every day of your stay in Italy special. They will show you Italy in a way that you would never see without their help. But only if you allow them to do so.

Yes, sometimes it's worth being vigilant and checking the bill to see if they added a couple of dishes you didn't order. Sometimes it's worth hanging your backpack in front of you, not behind you. Like when riding the Rome metro, for example. Or gripping your purse handle tighter while strolling along the Naples Bay waterfront, so a teenager on a lively "motorino" doesn't snatch it from your hands.

But not always. Many Italians are sincerely interested in where you're from, why you came to Italy, which places you plan to visit, which dishes are popular in your country, and how to cook them. And they will definitely praise your terrible Italian :)

In this chapter, there will be only one piece of advice: communicate. In broken Italian, broken English, gestures — any way you can.

Allow the Italians to make your First Time in Italy unforgettable. They will cope, you'll see.

By the way, if you want to understand the people who live here more deeply, you can read my second book. It's called The Italians. Just like the most important chapter of this book.

Here it is:

Point your phone's camera at the QR code,
and you'll find the book ;)

General info just in case

Capital of Italy: Rome

Currency: Euro

Population: 60.6 million people

Religion: Catholicism

Language: Italian

Form of government: parliamentary republic

Time zone: UTC+1 in winter and UTC+2 in summer

Time difference with other cities:

Washington: Italy is 6 hours ahead

Minneapolis: Italy is 7 hours ahead

Denver: Italy is 8 hours ahead

Los Angeles: Italy is 9 hours ahead

Ottawa: Italy is 6 hours ahead

London: Italy is 1 hour ahead

Canberra: Italy is 8 hours behind

Top 10 largest cities in Italy:

1. Rome

2. Milan

3. Naples

4. Turin

5. Palermo

6. Genoa

7. Bologna

8. Florence

9. Bari

10. Catania

If you are just starting to plan your route and still know little about Italian cities, the list below may come in handy. Choose according to your taste.

Walks through ancient Italian streets: Rome, Siena, Venice, Bologna, Verona

Art, painting, sculpture: Rome, Florence, Milan

Italian flavor with laundry hung between houses, scooters and noisy fish markets like in the movies: Naples, Palermo, Catania

Beach holiday and the clearest sea: the islands of Sicily and Sardinia, the regions of Campania and Apulia

Fashion and shopping: Milan, Rome

History of ancient Rome: Rome, Pompeii, Ercolano, Syracuse, Agrigento

Trekking: Trentino Alto Adige, Veneto, Umbria and Liguria regions

Large port cities: Genoa, Naples, Bari, Venice, Cagliari, Palermo, Ancona, Livorno

Unforgettable pizza and sweets: Naples

The most delicious fish cuisine: again Naples, Bari, Palermo, towns in the regions of Campania, Apulia and Sicily

Meat, steak, salami, smoked meats: Florence, towns of Tuscany and Umbria

Phone numbers to know

Single emergency number (police, ambulance, fire service): 112

U.S. Embassy in Rome: +39 06-46741 (from within Italy) or 011-39-06-46741 (from the U.S.)

U.S. Embassy in Milan: +39 02-290351 (from within Italy) or 011-39-02-290351 (from the U.S.)

U.S. Embassy in Naples: +39 081-583-8111 (from within Italy) or 011-39-081-583-8111 (from the U.S.)

British Embassy in Italy: +39 06-4220-0001 (from within Italy; select "2" between 9am and 5pm and "4" for emergencies outside these times) or +44 (0) 20-7008-5000 (from the U.K.)

Canadian Embassy in Italy: +39 06-85444-1 (from within Italy) or 613-996-8885 (from Canada)

Australian Embassy in Italy: +39 06 852721 (from within Italy), 1300 555 135 (within Australia) or +61 2 6261 3305 (from overseas)

Unexpected fines in Italy

► It is forbidden to remove sand, shells, and pebbles from beaches, with fines of up to 3,000 euros.

► Swimming in fountains is strictly prohibited, even during extreme heat (including dipping your feet in a fountain or bathing animals there), with fines of about 450 euros.

► You are not allowed to set up a tent anywhere you like; this is only permitted in designated campsites, with fines of about 300 euros.

► Smoking is strictly prohibited in restaurants, bars, and other establishments; it can only be done on the street (including at tables outside the restaurant or bar), with fines of about 250 euros.

Official museum websites

In Google, you will find many links to ticket reseller websites that may try to sell them to you at 2-3 times the original price. Therefore, buy tickets only from the official museum websites:

The Colosseum and
Roman Forum

Vatican Museums

Borghese Gallery
in Rome

Uffizi Gallery
in Florence

Brera Gallery
in Milan

Pantheon

Doge's Palace
in Venice

Milan Cathedral

Florence Cathedral

Leaning Tower
of Pisa

Official city transport apps

These apps will be useful if you are unable to purchase a paper bus ticket for any reason. Yes, the apps have low ratings and could be more user-friendly, but they are better than nothing.

Rome (iOS)

Rome (Android)

Milan (iOS)

Milan (Android)

Florence (iOS)

Florence (Android)

Venice (iOS)

Venice (Android)

Naples (iOS)

Naples (Android)

Italian signs

trattoria — a casual Italian restaurant serving traditional, home-style dishes

osteria — a simple, often rustic Italian eatery, offering local food

enoteca — a wine bar or shop focused on offering a variety of wines, often with light snacks

rosticceria — rotisserie

salumeria — a deli specializing in cured meats, cheeses, and other traditional deli products

prosciutteria — a specialty shop or eatery focused on serving and selling prosciutto and other cured meats, often paired with wine and traditional Italian snacks

panetteria — bakery

caffetteria — coffee shop

ristorante — restaurant

pescheria — fish market

macelleria — butcher shop

fruttivendolo — fruit and vegetable vendor

negozio di abbigliamento — clothing store

negozio di calzature / scarpe — shoe store

pelletteria / cuoiaio — leather goods store

tabaccheria — tobacco shop (here you can buy cigarettes, lottery tickets, public transportation tickets, and small items like pens or envelopes; sometimes, you can also print documents)

edicola — newsstand

libreria — bookstore

cartoleria — stationery store

farmacia — pharmacy

erboristeria — herbalist shop

profumeria — perfumery

parrucchiere — hairdresser

barbiere — barber

ferramenta — hardware store

copisteria — copy center

deposito bagagli — luggage storage

Your notes:

Have a nice trip!

Printed in Great Britain
by Amazon

55159383R00076